LOUIS PASTEUR

by Beverley Birch

Picture Credits
Anthony Blake Photo Library: 42; Bridgeman Art Library: 9, 34-35, 43, Giraudon front cover, 19, 26; John Cleare: 4; Mary Evans Picture Library: 8, 41; Exley Photographic Library: Nick Birch 12 (left), 16 (below both), 30, 31 (above), 35 (below), 38, 57 (both); Giraudon: Musée des Beaux-Arts, Nantes 25; Georges Goldner: 16 (above), 58 (below), 59; Hulton Picture Library: 40 (above), 45, 51; Illustrated London News: 11; The Mansell Collection: 55; Oxford Scientific Films: G.I. Bernard 47 (all); Pasteur Institute: 5, 15, 36, 40 (below), 61; Roger-Viollet: 50, 56; Ann Ronan Picture Library: 21, 28, 29, 44, 46 (all), 49, 54, 58 (above); Science Photo Library: 7, 20, 31 (below), CNRI 53 (below), Eric Grave 12-13, 53 (above), David Scharf 23, Sinclair Stammers 22, John Walsh, 33, 39.

Published in Great Britain in 1990 by
Exley Publications Ltd
16 Chalk Hill, Watford, Herts WD1 4BN, United Kingdom.

Text copyright © Beverley Birch, 1990
Copyright © Exley Publications, 1990

British Library Cataloguing in Publication Data
Birch, Beverley.
    Louis Pasteur. — (People who have helped the world).
    1. Chemistry. Pasteur, Louis. –
        Biographies – For children.
    I. Title.
    II. Series.
    540'.92'4

ISBN 1-85015-140-7

Series conceived and edited by Helen Exley.
Picture research: Karen Gunnell.
Research: Diana Briscoe.
Editorial: Margaret Montgomery.

Printed and bound in Hungary.

LOUIS PASTEUR

*The French chemist whose experiments on germs
led to the greatest medical breakthrough of all time*

Beverley Birch

≣EXLEY

Left and right: Louis Pasteur taught us to understand the enormous part microbes play in our lives. The dawn of understanding came when he proved that there are germs in the dusts of the air. Armed with germ-free flasks of soup, he went across France to Mont Blanc in the Alps, to show how few germs entered the flasks when he opened them in the clean mountain air.

Some scientists were certain he was wrong. Armed with their own flasks, they climbed the High Pyrenees to try and prove it. They failed.

The hunt for pure air

The procession wound its slow path up the mountain, the guides moving ahead with a surefooted tread on the stony track. Behind, the mule swayed beneath a load of strange, bulbous bottles. Around the plodding animal another man, a small, eager-faced man with glasses, ran this way and that, checked the harness, guided the animal anxiously along the edge of the precipice in the mistaken belief that he was less likeiy to slither off the narrow path than the sturdy little mule.

Up and up they toiled to the glinting peaks of snowy Mont Blanc. They sniffed the mountain air with excitement, (particularly that small, eager-eyed man, for surely, this was going to show he was right!) ... They climbed on and up in the morning sunshine – at last onto the white, untrodden snows of the Mer de Glace, the Sea of Ice.

And here, on the pure expanse of this great glacier, a strange kind of ceremony began. The man lit a lamp, a lamp with a powerful, jet-like flame. Delicately he removed a bottle from its cradle on the mule's back, and now it could be seen that it was not an ordinary bottle, but a plump round-bellied glass flask with an elegant straight, narrow neck tapering to a point.

He held it above his head. Inside there was a clear liquid which caught the light from snow and ice and sparkled.

With a pair of steel pincers he snapped off the tip of the fine glass neck. If you were close enough you could have heard a sharp hiss as air rushed through the narrow opening into the belly of the flask. Then almost immediately he took the lamp and ran its flame to and fro across the opening so

that the glass melted and the opening sealed again.

He took up the second flask: snap, that tell-tale hiss of air, swiftly the flame played across the opening ... then the third flask, the fourth, fifth ... each in turn, until twenty flasks had been opened and closed again.

And then he beamed. And they all beamed with him. Success!

It had to be right

Yesterday they had failed. They had toiled up that same path to that same glacier, to perform the same ceremony. But yesterday it had gone wrong.

Everything had gone according to plan until the moment came to seal the neck of the first flask with the lamp. Against the brilliance of the sky and snow-glare, it was impossible to see the flame! And the wind whipped it to and fro so there was no hope of aiming it at the open neck of the flask.

Only one answer: abandon the task and retrace their steps, find a tinker in the village of Chamonix at the foot of the mountain, get him to make a lamp that could give off a steady flame ... everything must be done exactly right. The flasks must be open only for an instant to let in the mountain air, and then closed again.

"I am the most hesitating of men, the most fearful of committing myself when I lack evidence. But on the contrary, no consideration can keep me from defending what I hold as true when I can rely on solid scientific evidence."
Louis Pasteur.

"Let me tell you the secret that has led me to the goal. My only strength resides in my tenacity."
Louis Pasteur.

The great debate

You may well wonder what was happening on that icy morning on the Mer de Glace. Louis Pasteur was proving something. Louis Pasteur was doing a precise and brilliantly simple scientific experiment. He was going to settle, once and for all, one of the major questions of science.

For weeks, he and his assistants had been preparing: cleaning flasks, making the liquid to put in them, boiling them, sealing them, packing them for their journeys. Some were carried across Paris to dank cellars or dusty yards, others were hoisted up a hill near Pasteur's home-town of Arbois, and others were nursed carefully on the train-journey to the Alps, for their voyage up Mont Blanc.

Louis Pasteur was trying to prove something,

and when Louis Pasteur looked for proof, he left nothing to chance.

"Always doubt yourself, till the facts cannot be doubted," Pasteur said. And there lies the secret of his enormous contribution to the world. However brilliant the idea, it is no good unless it *works:* so test and test again, with such attention to the tiniest of details, until there can be no question of any mistake.

There are a great deal of rather loose claims about Pasteur's work: he is said to have invented everything, from the smallest detail, like the special swan-necked flasks used in his early experiments, to single-handedly developing and proving the truth of the *germ theory of disease* – that the germs of those microscopic creatures known as microbes are the cause of many diseases. But to heap vague and often inaccurate claims like this upon him, is to obscure the man's real gigantic contribution to science and medicine.

Some of the scientific observations and ideas which Pasteur tackled had been around for a long time, some for two hundred years – since the first microscope revealed that vast world of tiny creatures which came to be known as microbes. But for all the notice scientists took of early observations about microbes, it was just as if Pasteur *was* the first.

The key to understanding disease

He certainly rediscovered things which some earlier scientists had already discovered. But Pasteur went further: he confirmed old and discovered new facts about microbes, but he also saw their interconnection. He made that visionary flight into understanding: not just microbes as fascinating things, but microbes as the root of many life processes of the world. Then he traced it by painstaking and imaginative experiment.

He made that inspired leap from seeing how microbes live and die, to realizing that here *was* the key to understanding disease. He became a prophet whose vision shot the scientists of his time forward into a revolutionary perception of the birth, life, decay and death of matter.

In this fifteenth-century German woodcut a man dies of the plague while the doctor wards off "evil emanations" with a sponge at his nose. Before Pasteur, people died in their hundreds of thousands without understanding why. The plague of 1346-49, the Black Death, killed perhaps half of Europe's population. In the plague of 1665, in London alone, one hundred thousand people died – at its height, six thousand a week.

After Pasteur's work, scientists could understand that the plague was a disease caused by a microbe – a bacterium – carried by rat fleas. They could begin the search for a cure, and for a way to prevent it.

Right: Year after year, people died in their hundreds of thousands from the epidemic diseases: cholera, typhoid, pneumonia, diphtheria, the plague, tuberculosis, syphilis. Before Pasteur's work on the germ theory of disease, doctors did not know what caused these illnesses, and could do nothing to prevent or cure them. Meanwhile the kind of poverty shown in this early picture of Paris – the overcrowding, filth and damp, the dirty food and water – continued to spread the microbes of these killer diseases.

Opposite page: Mothers died in childbirth; children died in infancy – it was common for one family to lose two or three children. Whole families died in epidemics: people could be dead within six hours of falling ill with cholera. There was no explanation, no treatment and no hope. (Painting by Henry Jules Jean Geoffroy, 1853-1924.)

Armed with this perception they were able to unlock the secrets of disease. Doctors became not merely those who helped people to endure and perhaps survive disease, but those who *cured* and *prevented* illnesses which had been the scourge of humankind for thousands of years.

In the decades that followed whole new sciences were born. The first was the science of *microbiology.* The scientific study of the cause, control and prevention of disease also developed, not least through *inoculation* and *immunization*. (These are the techniques which encourage the body to develop its own immunity to microbes). There was also *asepsis* – the control and destruction of germs in hospitals, particularly in surgery.

Pasteur and those he trained were in the forefront of this great movement in science and medicine: their work revolutionized medical practice, and their discoveries were an inspiration to scientists and doctors throughout the world: an influence whose scale is so vast that it can never be fully measured.

And as he galloped down this path, on the way Pasteur rescued whole industries from disaster – possibly from extinction – with his researches in

wine and beer, silkworms, cattle and sheep diseases.

Nowadays, we all depend on *pasteurization,* the technique which bears his name and which most often reminds us of him. Daily, dairies free our milk from disease-causing germs using this process.

Enemies

Not surprisingly, he provoked enemies: his work, particularly as a standard-bearer of the germ theory of disease, disproved some long-held theories, and such was his conviction that he rode rough-shod over those who refused to respond to the truth of his researches, or who picked holes in his results.

With hindsight, and the greater knowledge of modern science, we can see that there were some holes to be found. But how few, and comparatively how vast was the forward march of science and medicine in which Pasteur's work was one of the great motive forces!

So what was he trying to prove on that glacier on Mont Blanc? It was something that is so commonplace to us now that one wonders why, for over a hundred years, scientists had been arguing about it. It was quite simply the question of whether there are germs in the air.

It is perhaps hard now to think of this as a revolutionary idea, for in our everyday life we accept it by using soaps and antiseptic cleaners, by the way we clean and dress wounds, in the fact that hospitals do their best to perform operations in germ-free conditions with germ-free instruments.

We now know that there *are* microscopic living organisms on and in everything in the world – on solid matter, floating in the dusts of the air, in water and other liquids. We know that some of these micro-organisms do essential tasks for us: they make waste materials decay to provide food for plant life; they turn raw materials into bread or wine; some even take part in the digestive process in our bodies. We also know that others cause disease when they enter the human, animal or plant body, and can kill, slaughtering people or animals in their millions.

"In all the immensity of creation, I have taken my drop of water and I have taken it full of rich jelly – that is, to use the language of science, full of elements most suited to the development of small beings. And I wait, I observe, I question it, I beg it to be so kind as to begin over again just to please me, the primitive act of creation; it would be so fair a sight! But it is mute! It has been mute for years. Ah! That is because I have kept far from it, and still keep far from it, the only thing that it has not been given to man to produce. I have kept from it the germs that float in the air; I have kept from it life, for life is a germ and a germ is life. Never will the belief in spontaneous generation arise from the mortal blow that this simple experiment has given it."

Pasteur, in a public lecture at the Sorbonne.

None of this was known when Pasteur began his probing into the mysteries of germs. All that *was* known was that these creatures existed.

We have a Dutchman, Leeuwenhoek, who died a hundred years before Pasteur was born, to thank for that. Leeuwenhoek had an enormous curiosity about the world around him. He wanted to find out what things *really* looked like, and he heard that a magnifying lens would help. So he set out to learn how to grind and polish lenses, and began a life of peering and sniffing and poking at everything he could lay his hands on, just to find out … skin, hair, tree-bark, seeds, insects, the cavities of rotten teeth, all were victims of the prying glint of his lenses.

A cholera epidemic in Granada in 1887. At its worst five hundred people were dying each day. Here people are burning fires of tar and sulphur in a vain attempt to disinfect the streets. By this time scientists knew cholera was caused by a microbe, and the microbe had been identified. It was also known that it was carried mainly by water infected by cholera victims. But this knowledge was only the first step to controlling the disease.

The microscope

In fact, he had invented what we call the microscope, and from his quiet life in a small Dutch town towards the end of the seventeenth century, he set the world on fire. For the first time people realized there was this world of creatures so tiny that they

11

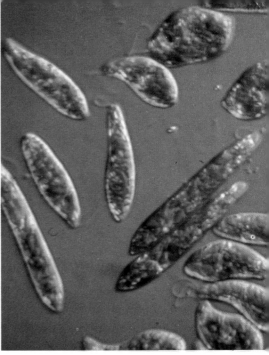

Above: Pasteur's last microscope. The microscope was at the heart of his work: through Pasteur we learned of the innumerable useful and dangerous tasks that microbes perform in the world. In his hands the microscope was transformed for all time from merely a tool of observation into a weapon wielded tirelessly against disease and infection.

were invisible to the naked eye.

Peering one day through one of his magnifying lenses, he was transfixed by the sight of millions of tiny creatures in the rainwater in his yard! How they slithered and wriggled ... no matter how long he watched them, they never stopped. A thousand times smaller than anything you could see with the naked eye! Millions of them: a thousand times smaller even than the eye of a large louse (and a whole louse is too small to be seen ...)

Everything he looked at was swarming with these tiny creatures. He did not make guesses about what they were doing, and it never entered his head that they were *causing* anything – least of all decay or disease. But he did discover that they were killed by heat: one day he was squinting at scrapings from his own teeth, and found that after he'd drunk scalding hot coffee, the creatures were either dead or very sluggish.

He wrote his findings down and sent long descriptions to scientists in England: they had recently formed the Royal Society to exchange scientific ideas and learn from each other. He told them he could *grow* these creatures in water mixed with

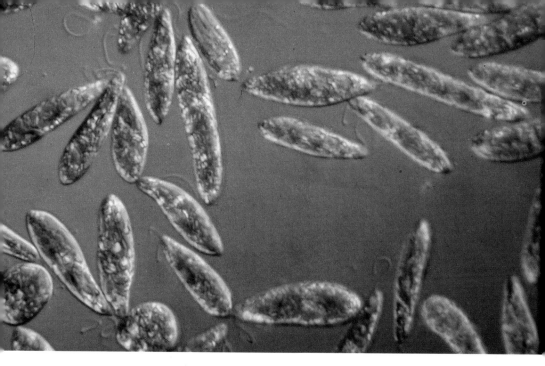

pepper: one drop of pepper-water held more than two million seven-hundred-thousand! They built microscopes, repeated his experiments and found he told the truth.

Spallanzani's work on microbes

But after Leeuwenhoek's discoveries and that first excitement, the little creatures were on the brink of being forgotten again. Leeuwenhoek was dead and the eighteenth century well past the half-way mark, when an Italian priest named Spallanzani, a professor at the University of Reggio in Italy, became fascinated by the wiggling microscopic beings.

In Spallanzani's time there was a great debate going on: it was the same debate that, about one hundred years later, would fire Louis Pasteur into the front line of battle as its fierce warrior, to settle the matter once and for all.

The question was this: does every living thing have to have parents, or can living things spring into life *spontaneously?* The argument was bound up with people's belief in how the world was first formed.

Above: A modern picture of the kind of micro-organisms Leeuwenhoek might have seen in stagnant water using his microscopes. These are single-celled protozoa. Protozoa of various kinds are found widely in damp places. They looked amazing, but it would not be until Pasteur's work that anything about them would be applied to preventing disease.

13

Spontaneous life?

The popular idea in Spallanzani's day (and it remained so until Pasteur laid it to rest), was that things *did* come alive spontaneously. If you buried the carcass of a bullock – so the story went – out would pop a spontaneously-generated swarm of bees! Wasps and beetles would emerge out of dung, mice and frogs slither from the slime of river banks, and maggots from meat.

Spallanzani thought this whole idea was ridiculous. But how could he show he was right? One day he read the writings of a man named Redi, who had proved that flies had to *reach* meat for the maggots to appear, and that if you stopped flies getting to the meat (by covering it) – no maggots!

Spallanzani was entranced by the simplicity of this. Not just observe, but *experiment,* find proof. So he began his experiments and showed that the tiny living creatures we now call microbes do not arise spontaneously, that when you find them *on* things or *in* liquids, it is because they have reached there from somewhere else.

He did an experiment very like one Pasteur devised many years later, to prove the same point: he boiled soups of seeds and beans for an hour to kill all microbes, sealed the necks of the flasks by melting the glass, and showed that no new microbes appeared inside the flasks. They could not enter because of the sealed neck.

Microbes divide

He read that a Swiss scientist named de Saussure had seen that microbes increased by multiplying – each one split into two, and those two into four, and so on.

Enchanted by this idea Spallanzani found a way to trap one in a drop of distilled water, and then watched it through the microscope until he actually saw it happening. The tiny rod-like shape got thinner and thinner in the middle, until it became two small rods held together by no more than a cobweb-thin thread! Some frantic jerks and wriggles, and before his eyes they had pulled apart and were *two* rod-like creatures … and then it happened again! Each one grew thin in the middle …

But in the end, in spite of the excitement that Spallanzani's work caused in the learned societies of Europe, the novelty of peering into this world of the infinitely small wore off. No one learned much that was new, and interest in the creatures faded. As the years went by, those old theories that Spallanzani had worked so hard to bury, the theories about the *spontaneous generation* of living things, reared their argumentative heads again.

And then the germ theory

Then came Louis Pasteur, in France. Within thirty years, the knowledge of the world was transformed. Pasteur, with his passionate convictions and meticulous experiments, propelled scientists from the darkness of prejudice, and half-knowledge, into the daylight in which all the techniques of modern preventive medicine could be born.

An engraving of young Louis Pasteur.

Louis Pasteur unquestionably proved, and scientists grasped the idea, that the germs of microbes do not arise spontaneously but travel into things (matter and liquids) from outside – for example in the dusts of the air. Once he'd done that, the way was open to proving the *germ theory of disease*, that much disease is caused by the invasion of the human, animal, or plant body by microbes which overwhelm and weaken it.

The scientists of Pasteur's day were not slow to grasp the nettle: if microbes caused many diseases, then the microbes must be tracked and caught, and ways found of controlling, killing or preventing them from taking hold. The era of immunology was born, the knowledge of how to make the body develop its own defences against the microbes of specific diseases.

How many countless lives have been saved by this great movement in medicine of which Pasteur was one of the prime movers, a great inspirer of other great men who have worked to clear the world of the diseases which only a little more than a hundred years ago wiped out people in their hundreds of thousands each year.

Above: Arbois, where Louis grew up in a house which was also his father's tannery, on the banks of the river Cuisance. The family house in this small country town remained his place of retreat throughout his life. It was also in Arbois and the surrounding area that he did much of his research on wine and beer fermentation.

Right: Louis did these two pastels of his father (right) and his mother (below) when he was sixteen; they now hang in the Pasteur Institute in Paris. As a boy, Louis loved to draw – in pencil, charcoal or chalks; and by the age of thirteen he was showing a noticeable talent in his sketches of family and friends, the house and the river, and the surrounding fields. Yet Louis' ambition was not to become an artist: he wanted to be a teacher.

To appreciate this revolutionary contribution to the world, we need to go back to Louis Pasteur's beginnings, to trace the story as he and his fellow workers saw it, as the world saw it at the time.

Pasteur the boy

The early life of Louis Pasteur is remarkable for the absence of anything to warn us that he was going to be a scientist. He showed no particular early interest in science, nor was there anything to give us a clue that he would become an explorer, a searcher for some of the fundamental secrets of life, or a man with so strong a sense of mission.

His talents seemed mainly in drawing and painting; at the age of thirteen he showed a remarkable skill in pictures of his sisters and mother and drawings of the river that ran by his home in Arbois.

He grew up in that part of France which is not far from Switzerland and the Alps, in the area of the Jura mountains which form a rugged barrier between the two countries. Here, in the small town of Dôle on the river Doubs, he was born, on December 27, 1822, in a house on a street that now bears his name. But in 1822 it was called the Rue des Tanneurs – the street of the tanners; each house was a tannery where the fresh skins of cattle and sheep were "tanned" and turned into leather. Louis' father was a tanner.

But Louis was little more than three years old when he and his sisters were loaded into a cart with their furniture and their father's tools, to make the journey to the south east. They settled in the town of Arbois, snug amongst its wooded hills; here there was a tannery, a house with pits in the yard where the skins could be soaked, a room for his father to sell leather, another for his workshop, and space for the family to live above.

Here, with his three sisters, Louis grew up. Hilly Arbois with its plane-trees and poplars, its squares and shady arcades, its little river Cuisance running by the wall of his house and splashing under the bridge, and its nearby fields where small boys could play and fish endlessly ... this town remained the focus of his young life for many years.

To Paris

He seems to have developed one overriding, early ambition – to become a teacher and go to Paris to study at the Ecole Normale Supérieure, a school founded by Napoleon to train professors for the schools and colleges of France.

But Louis' first attempt at studying in Paris was disastrous. He was sixteen, and the bonds that held him to his family were too strong. Plucked from the familiar haunts of his country life and plunged four hundred kilometres away into the crowded streets and looming houses of Paris, he was crippled with homesickness. He did not see the excitement of the Latin Quarter, the students thronging the university of the Sorbonne and pavement cafés humming with young people. He felt only the difference and the loneliness.

The experiment lasted for only six weeks, before his father made the long journey by stage-coach to fetch him home again. Back went Louis to the college at Arbois, and back to his drawings and paintings. He began producing a remarkable set of pastel portraits of friends and acquaintances. Later he went to college in Besançon, only forty kilometres away instead of four hundred. There he seems to have flourished, been happy, and much praised for his drawing.

But he seems never to have lost sight of his goal. At Besançon he began to prepare for the Ecole Normale. He was not content with his first results in the entrance exam, for though he got a place there, he came fifteenth out of twenty-two. He decided to leave Besançon, study for another year, and try again.

Paris again

So Louis went back to Paris, and this was very different from his first miserable experience. Here was a Louis determined and ready to reach his goal. He lived at the Barbet school, the same that he had tried so many years earlier. Here he was a teacher as well as a student, giving lessons to the younger boys from six until seven in the morning.

Jean Béraud 1889

And then the day began, with other lessons at the famous school called the Lycée St. Louis, and after, the jewels of his day, those lectures at the University of the Sorbonne.

It is about now that we can detect the seeds of Louis' future taking root: we find him passing out of the great halls of the Sorbonne, amidst the crowds of six or seven hundred students all chattering about the latest lecture, and we find Louis spellbound by the vistas opening before him.

What a lecturer this chemistry professor, Monsieur Dumas, was! What a world of fascination he opened up! Louis wrote excited letters about these lectures, and it seems as if the grip of that first excitement never left him ... nor the friendship of Professor Dumas.

At the end of the school year Louis came fourth in the exam for the Ecole Normale. He was so eager to begin that he arrived before the beginning of term. So in October 1843, shortly before his twenty-first birthday, Louis entered the Ecole Normale to learn to teach chemistry and physics.

Above: When Louis arrived in Paris in 1842 to begin his studies for the Ecole Normale, he was struck by the vastness and variety of the city, with its appalling contrast between great wealth and miserable poverty. He little realized that this vibrant city would claim him for nearly all his remaining long and active life. Nor did he foresee what a turbulence of ideas he himself would begin among the scientists of its great university, the Sorbonne, and the communities of students in the surrounding Latin Quarter. (Painting by Jean Beraud, 1849-1936.)

19

First explorations on his own

Microbes couldn't have been further from his mind as he came to the end of his studies at the Ecole Normale and looked around for something special to study, something to give him a chance for independent explorations.

He *must* become a first-rate teacher: his heart was set on it. He must understand everything he would teach so thoroughly that he could fire youngsters with enthusiasm, just as Professor Dumas had captured him during those lectures in the Sorbonne. And perhaps it was his artist's eye that drew him to crystals – they are such delicately intricate fragments.

To Louis' fascination, one of his teachers had shown him a specimen of a salt which had formed crystals; but although it was apparently a very pure salt, it was actually a mixture of three different kinds of crystals. Louis was intrigued. Why three? There must be some purpose ... a thousand questions buzzed in his brain – a searching for some reason why nature arranged things like this.

And like every scientist since the dawn of our search to know the world around us, he was in his own way launched on that most fundamental of questions in science: what *are* substances made of; how can we work out how matter is built?

Crystals and light

Crystals had attracted the attention of the curious for thousands of years. By Louis' time scientists knew a lot about what they *looked* like, but not a great deal more. Louis' elderly physics teacher, Professor Biot, had also found out that if a beam of light is shone through some crystals, the beam of light doesn't continue in the same straight path, it *bends*.

Why? Louis was even more intrigued. You must remember that this was long before scientists had worked out how the building blocks of substances – what we call the *atoms* – are arranged in each substance. It was several decades before they were able to understand how a group of atoms is arranged

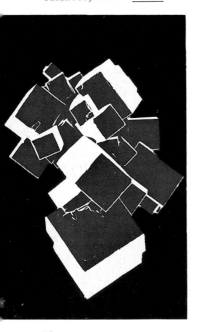

Crystals of pure salt, like those which so fascinated Louis and prompted him to begin a study of crystals. Here, they are magnified by an electron microscope, which is vastly more powerful than the microscopes Louis was using. The picture shows clearly the regular pattern in the structures of atoms and molecules in the crystals, and the variety of crystal shapes, always with a series of flat, many-sided surfaces, called facets.

to form a *molecule,* and how an arrangement of molecules in its turn makes up the substance – a solid, gas or liquid. And it was more than half a century before the discovery of radioactivity began to reveal the *inner* structure of the atom.

So the fact that crystals did unexpected things with beams of light was interesting. It made Louis wonder if there was a link between the *kind* of crystal and what it did to light. Or between the crystal's *chemical composition* – its combination of ingredients or what scientists call its *compounds* – and what it did to light. Or, between its *shape* and what it did to light. There was enough new here to take him well off into uncharted territory. He began making a careful study of a very beautiful series of compounds, called tartaric acid and the tartrates. Two forms of tartaric acid crystals were found in the encrustations which build up inside wine barrels while grape juice ferments. But there was a mystery: if you made a solution with the first type of crystal in water, it bent a beam of light, as Professor Biot had seen.

But if you made a water solution with the second type of crystal, it did *not* bend the beam of light! Yet both crystals were *identical* chemically – that is they were both made up of exactly the same ingredients.

The first adventure

There must be something here: his developing explorer's nose could scent it!

And off set Louis Pasteur on this first of his adventures, prodding and picking over piles of crystals, looking at them first this way, then that through his magnifying glass, measuring the angles between the different faces, dissolving them, forming them again, struggling to find something that would explain this extraordinary difference in what they did to light.

He couldn't find it. But with what determination he pressed on – beyond the point where many young scientists in their first piece of research would have given in to weary disenchantment.

Jean-Baptiste Dumas, Louis' Professor of Chemistry at the Sorbonne, and his life-long friend. It was the excitement of Professor Dumas' lectures that first awoke Louis' fascination with science. Throughout Louis' scientific work, it was scientists like Dumas who recognized the importance of Louis' work, and gave him support and encouragement.

Tartaric acid crystals – the crystals found in wine vats when grape juice is fermenting.

The first discovery

And he found himself in the middle of his first great discovery: peering for the thousandth time through his magnifying glass, it struck him that the crystals which treated light so differently were the same in *all but one respect*. The difference was so subtle that he hadn't seen it before! All the faces, or facets, of the two kinds of crystal were identical – *except one*. In one form of the crystal one of the facets sloped one way: in the other it sloped the other way.

With mounting excitement, he dissolved the different crystals separately in solutions of water, and predicted what each would do to a beam of light. Was he going to be right? He hardly dared hope!

He was, and with a burst of glee, he realized what he had discovered and he rushed out to find the first person he could tell ...

What was so important in all this about acids and the facets of crystals and the beam of light? It meant something very significant, for it showed to Louis that you could study the *structure* of a crystal, by studying what it did with a beam of light; that investigating how a crystal *behaved,* could tell you something of how it was *built!*

In these days when the investigation of how substances were built was still in its infancy, it was as though a gate opened. Louis' discovery suggested new methods, new techniques, a whole new approach. In the next years Louis was busily engaged in this work, in effect laying the foundations of a new science, the science of *stereochemistry.*

So Louis' discovery was a scientific leap of some significance. And it marked the young man out as an explorer of quality, with the determination and the methodical persistence of a first-class scientist, but also with the glorious instincts of an adventurer ...

All kinds of other questions buzzed in Louis' brain. These crystals were alike, except that they were mirror images of each other. Again, why? There was a reason for this difference (scientists call it *dissymetry*); nature used it in some way, but what way? These questions were to absorb Louis happily for the next ten years, until an unexpected turn of events propelled him from the world of crystals into the world of another, quite different phenomenon ...

Madame Pasteur

By the end of 1848 Louis' time at the Ecole Normale was over, and by January of 1849 he was installed in his first big job: lecturer in chemistry at the University of Strasbourg. It was here, at the age of twenty-six, that he met and fell in love with Marie Laurent, daughter of the university principal.

Fifteen days later, with that precision of purpose and determination so characteristic of Louis, he wrote to the principal asking for Marie's hand in marriage. "My family is comfortable, but not rich," he wrote. "All we possess is not worth more than fifty thousand francs, and I have long ago decided to let my sisters have it all ... All I possess is good health, a willing spirit, and my work.

"I have been a Doctor of Science for eighteen months and I have presented a few works to the

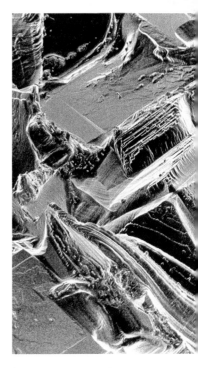

Sea salt crystals shown here magnified one hundred times by an electron microscope. This was not developed until the 1930s. It can produce images of structures up to a million times smaller than the human eye can see.

"I woke up every morning with the thought that you wouldn't return my love, and then I wept! My work means nothing to me – to me, who was so devoted to my crystals that when I went to bed I wished the night was not so long, so that I could get back to work quicker!"

Louis, in a letter to Marie Laurent before their marriage.

23

Academy of Science which have been well received ... As to the future, all I can say is that, unless my tastes change entirely, I shall devote myself to chemical research."

He seems to have felt that Marie's mother needed persuading, for he wrote to her, "There is nothing in me to attract a young girl's fancy, but my memory tells me that those who have known me very well have loved me very much."

Yet he seems not to have been at all confident of the answer he would get from Marie. He pleaded with her, "All that I ask, Mademoiselle, is that you will not be hasty in your judgment of me. You might make a mistake. Time will show you that, under a cold and shy outside, which doubtless displeases you, there is a heart full of affection for you."

They were married on May 29, 1849. From the beginning Marie seems to have accepted Louis' overwhelming absorption in his work, and to have grown used to a husband whose mind bubbled with the events of his laboratory. She devoted her life to supporting him, freeing him from household cares, helping him and loving him, and allowing him complete freedom for his research.

But she was also much more than a homemaker for him. Emile Roux, one of Pasteur's pupils who later became famous for his own work, tells how she discussed his work, spurred his thinking on, and was therefore one of the best of his scientific collaborators.

So Louis settled to married life, and for the next five years they lived at Strasbourg. Louis was absorbed with his crystals and his teaching. Marie added to her role as wife and collaborator the demands of a mother, for at Strasbourg three of their five children were born: daughter Jeanne, followed a year later by a son, Jean-Baptiste, and two years later, baby Cecile.

To Lille, as professor of chemistry

September of 1854: a new challenge! Louis was made professor of chemistry and Dean of the new Faculty of Science at Lille – a prosperous industrial city in the north of France where a great many gentlemen were in the trade of fermenting beetroot juice to make alcohol.

Louis was just thirty-two and very young for a position of such responsibility. It was an outstanding achievement. He took his teaching seriously: he wanted to infuse his students with the same sense of awe in the infinite realm of nature's miracles that he felt. "Has anybody a son," he exhorted a gathering of prosperous manufacturers and their wives, "who would not be interested if you gave him a potato and told him 'from that potato you can make sugar, from sugar you can make alcohol, from alcohol vinegar'?"

The students of Lille were interested. Louis Pasteur's lectures were events not to be missed. He swept his pupils off on energetic tours of the factories and foundries, steel and metal works of France and Belgium.

The problem of the sour alcohol

Then came the day in 1856, when Monsieur Bigo asked for his advice. Monsieur Bigo was one of those manufacturers of alcohol from beet sugar (and also the father of one of Louis' pupils), and he had a problem: most of the time the process of changing beet sugar into alcohol in his factory was going well. But in some of the vats the juice wasn't turning into alcohol, it was just going sour. The spoiled vats were losing Monsieur Bigo thousands of francs a day.

Louis didn't know anything about alcohol manufacture and fermentation. He'd had some thoughts on fermentation, for his studies revolved around crystals found in wine barrels during fermentation. But really no one knew anything much about it, except that it happened, and they had known that for thousands of years: you could take various crops, let them ferment, and turn them into alcholic drinks like wine and beer. But no one knew what caused this.

Monsieur Bigo hoped that a man of science like his son's teacher might have some new suggestion,

Vast numbers of people worked in France's famous wine industry. But each year, a great proportion of the harvest would be wasted – something was going drastically wrong in the fermentation process. The same troubles existed in the beer industry. The losses were causing many businesses to fail.
Louis Pasteur turned his mind to these problems and was able to come up with the solution. And this, in turn, would lead to his greatest discoveries in the field of medicine. (Painting by Edouard Debat-Ponsan.)

so Louis went along to the factory to have a look. He sniffed at the vats of fermenting sugar-beet juice. Here were the ones where the juice was turning to alcohol.

And here it was a very different matter. In these vats there was a slimy sour mess! Louis peered at it, but was none the wiser. He decided he'd better have a closer look, properly, in his laboratory. So he put some of the sour stuff into bottles, and like the careful scientist he was, he also took some of the good stuff, and off he went.

Under the microscope

Under his microscope went a drop of liquid from a good vat. What was he looking for? He didn't really know. Perhaps there would be some familiar crystals that would start him on a track to understanding this fermentation process. Perhaps because the well-trained scientist in him said: have a good, long, hard, considered look before you do anything else.

At once, with the magnifying power of the microscope, he saw that the tiny drop of liquid was filled with *minute* globules, little yellowish round and oval shapes that swarmed with darker specks. They were far smaller than any crystal he had ever seen! He searched his memory for some clue as to what they were, and then from one of those little corners of his mind he dragged the realization that these must be the yeast cells which scientists knew were always in the mixture when sugar-beet juice or grapes were fermenting.

Scientists knew they were there: but they did not agree what they were doing there. There were several ideas: some believed the yeast cells were a substance that was rotting and as it did so it split the sugar molecules in sugar-beet or grape juice into alcohol and the clear gas called *carbon dioxide*.

The yeast was alive!

But the more Louis watched, the more he became convinced, with a mounting excitement, that the yeast globules were *alive,* and that the yeasts were

"Chance in one guise or another, has frequently attended the birth of discovery. Chance evidence comes to everybody, but only a genius is capable of interpreting it correctly. Genius is not enough. Without adequate scientific training, even the most intelligent individual remains incapable of interpreting the play of accidental factors, and incapable of experimentally reproducing some phenomena which chance has thrown in his way, so as to ascertain whether his deductions are valid or not."

Hilaire Cuny, from *"Louis Pasteur, his theories"*.

somehow at the bottom of this fermentation process – that they were *doing* it!

He also had a half-memory about other scientists in Germany who thought the yeasts were alive, and a scientist named Cagniard-Latour in France who had poked around in beer breweries and reported that he had seen little buds on the yeasts ...

Louis peered through his microscope again. Yes! He could see the buds. Hour after hour he watched, utterly absorbed in this miniature world, and then first one, then another bud grew larger, and then split away, and there were two yeast globules where there had been only one.

He'd actually seen it! And it dawned on him that he also understood what was happening: the yeasts were growing and multiplying, and as they did so they were feeding on the beet-juice and giving off alcohol and carbon dioxide!

But this still didn't solve his problem, Monsieur Bigo's problem: why were some of the vats sour? He went back to his peering. A drop of the slimy stuff under the microscope. No nice round globules of yeast. He looked harder. Definitely none. He

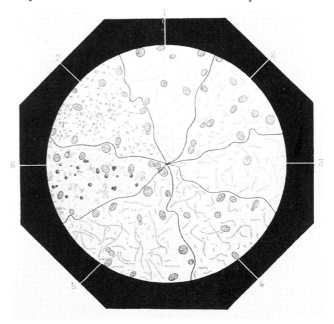

Louis' work in the sugar beet factory was only the beginning of many years of work on fermentation. He showed that microbes cause fermentation in many different substances. This is a sketch by Louis Pasteur from his Studies on Beer, published in 1876. It shows the micro-organisms which cause fermentation in various types of liquids – including spoiled wine, vinegar and soured milk.

picked up the bottle and had a good look at it. There *were* specks stuck to the inside and floating in the liquid ...

The black rods

Any in the healthy stuff? He checked. No. With some difficulty he managed to get one of the specks into a drop of pure water and under his microscope. He stared in disbelief. Tiny black rods, millions and millions of minute black rods in this single drop of water, busy in some kind of weird, shimmering dance that never stopped. Much smaller than yeasts: he tried to work out how big each was. It couldn't be more than one twenty-five thousandth of an inch long!

More hours went by, as Louis, like Leeuwenhoek and Spallanzani, fell under the spell of these creatures. Back to the factory, quick: nothing else mattered now except to follow his explorer's nose after these dancing rods. More samples: yes, the sourer the fermentation had become, the more of these creatures were in it.

And he understood what was happening. These creatures had overrun the yeast cells and stopped them making alcohol; instead the little rod-like fellows were manufacturing *lactic acid:* the same ingredient that makes milk sour.

But his instincts as a scientist did not falter. Don't jump to conclusions: make sure. Back to the beet factory again. More samples. Rods? Yes! Always, when the vats had turned sour, the rods were there. And when they were there, there was no alcohol, only *the acid of sour milk.*

The alcohol industry is saved

He couldn't say how they got into the vats, or from where (although even as early as this in his work on microbes, he had a strong suspicion it was from the air), but he was able to tell Monsieur Bigo how to make sure he would get good alcohol: test the liquid from the vats under a microscope. If only yeast cells could be seen, all would be well, but if even *one* of the rod-like creatures had made an

Louis' research on fermentation led him, over the next twenty years, to develop ways of stopping wine, vinegar and beer from spoiling – the technique we know as pasteurization. This is an engraving of apparatus Louis used in his experiments on beer. The flask on the left contained the <u>wort</u> (the ingredients which, after fermentation, became beer). This was boiled to kill the microbes. The flask on the right contained a pure yeast culture. Air could enter only through the tube. The apparatus was left like this for eighteen months, and the beer remained sound because no microbes could travel up the tube.

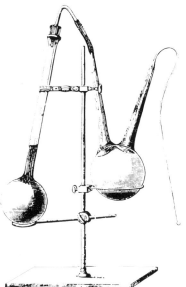

The equipment developed by Louis Pasteur to pasteurize beer. The technique he developed is now widely used not only for wine and beer, but also for milk, milk products and other food stuffs: it is part of Louis Pasteur's enormous legacy to our health. Yet neither he nor any other scientists of his era worked in large laboratories equipped with the latest technology. Their equipment was basic, their laboratories unwanted attics or cellars, their resources little more than their own skill and ingenuity and the knowledge they shared and exchanged with their fellow scientists.

appearance: throw it all away, destroy every bit of it. Once into the juice, the black rods would multiply into millions and wipe out the yeast cells.

To the alcohol manufacturers of Lille, Louis was a hero. Their industry was saved from ruin, and there were many families who must have thanked Louis, that year of 1856. But in the pages of history, the world had much more to thank Louis for.

This experience in Bigo's sugar-beet factory had set his feet on a track from which he would never be shaken.

He couldn't put these creatures out of his mind. He was certain that the rods *caused* the sour milk acid and the yeasts *caused* the alcohol. A picture took hold of his mind: rods and yeasts doing battle with each other. It was a picture which never left him and drove him ever on to his work on the microbes of disease.

Microbes

He couldn't study the rods properly all tangled up in the pulp of sugar-beet. His first task must be to find something they would grow in, in which he could see them clearly.

He tried sugar first, mixed with water, for he knew there was always sugar in fermenting liquid. It was no good. They were very particular in their tastes, these dancing rods! He turned himself into a scientific cook, trying all sorts of mixtures, heating and filtering, and then sowing his rods, and finding, with disappointment, that they did not grow. ...

What about a soup made with yeast? He tried it: he put dried yeast into water and added a little sugar, carefully measured. Then he boiled it so that it would be completely free of any microbes (he knew microbes were killed by heat), and he strained the soup till it was perfectly clear so there would be nothing to stop him watching the little rods ...

Now would the rods taken from the sick fermentations in Bigo's factory grow if they were left in this clear, germ-free yeast soup? He put a speck from a sick fermentation into a flask of the soup, and then carried the flask to his incubating oven where the mixture could be kept comfortably warm.

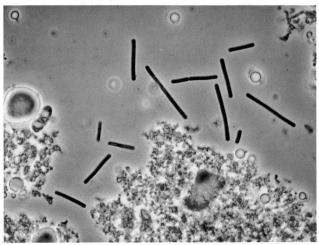

Above: Modern stainless
steel wine vats are
controlled by the latest
computer technology.
Pasteur's pasteurization
principle used is still
exactly the same: the
destruction of microbes
that would spoil the wine
by using exactly the right
amount of heat, enough to
kill the microbes, but not
to spoil the wine.

Louis Pasteur's "dancing
black rods" – the bacillus
he detected in the spoiled
sugar beet vats. They are
shown here in yogurt.

An anxious day passed, filled with a thousand other tasks demanded of this busy teacher, who also played an important role for the manufacturers and farmers of Lille: they relied so heavily on his advice about fertilizers and manures ... But whenever he peeped into his incubator at the flask, nothing was happening. He *almost* began to feel discouraged; yet he was certain, so certain, that his guess was right.

And then, when the waiting had stretched to two interminable days, he saw something – bubbles, little puffs of gas, curling up through the soup. He squinted in the half-light, hardly daring to hope. They were coming from the speck he had sown! But – surely there were specks which hadn't been there yesterday!

Black rods, by the million

Under the microscope went a drop of the liquid – and he stared in sheer ecstasy! Millions of rods! The speck had spawned others ... and – he checked, meticulously careful – yes, the same acid had appeared in his yeast soup – *the acid of sour milk.*

But caution! There must be no jumping to conclusions without absolute proof! He took some rods from this yeast soup and put it in more yeast soup, freshly-boiled and germ-free, and he waited again. The same thing happened. Each rod grew longer and longer and then split and became *two* rods where there had been one ...

He put some in fresh milk. The milk soured and the rods multiplied. He did it again and again, till he was certain beyond any doubt. If he added a tiny drop of rods to a clear soup, millions of new rods *always* appeared and they *always* made the acid of sour milk.

The mystery is solved

He had solved the mystery of fermentation, that mystery which had remained unexplained for ten thousand years! These minute creatures were the *cause* of the fermentation. Just as yeast was the cause of the fermentation which changed sugar into

"To believe one has discovered an important scientific fact, to long to announce it, and yet to restrain oneself for days, weeks, sometimes even years; to strive to disprove one's own experiments; to publish one's discovery only after exhausting every alternative possibility – yes, the task is a hard one. But when ... certainty is reached, the reward is one of the keenest joys of which the human soul is capable."
Louis Pasteur.

alcohol, so these rods were the cause of the fermentation which produced lactic acid.

When he was absolutely certain, by August of 1857, he told everyone about it: he read a paper about it to the Lille Scientific Society; he told his students that fermentation was a living process, caused by microscopic living creatures performing a giant's work, and the students were enthralled. He wrote to his old teacher, Dumas, and prepared a statement for the Academy of Science in Paris, the pinnacle of scientific society in France, where reports on science throughout the world were read and discussed.

There was much excitement. Louis' conclusions flew in the face of the theories of several of the most respected scientists. They believed that fermentation was no more than a chemical reaction between substances when they were added together. We now know they were partly right: it is a substance *produced* by the yeast which causes alcoholic fermentation through a chemical reaction.

But how much more right was Louis, insisting that without yeast, a living organism, no alcoholic fermentation would take place!

Louis' work on fermentation went on for many years: he showed that microbes cause fermentation in many different substances; he also developed ways of preventing wine, vinegar and beer from spoiling, by killing harmful microbes with heat. This is the process named after him – *pasteurization*. Nowadays, every glass of pasteurized milk or yoghourt, healthy and germ-free, is a testimony to Louis Pasteur.

Foreseeing the germ theory

His studies on fermentation made Louis convinced that microbes were at the root of a host of other useful tasks in the world – and at the heart of a thousand dangerous things too. One day, one day, he would show it …

At the end of 1857 a new era had begun in his life: he was called back to his old school, the Ecole Normale in Paris, to become Administrator and

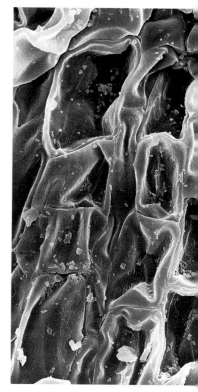

Wine yeast on the surface of a wine bottle cork. The yeast shows up as tiny balls against the cork, while the structure of the cork is also revealed by the power of a modern microscope. Pasteur would not have seen such detail, for the electron microscope was only developed over fifty years later.

"Nothing is more agreeable to a man who has made science his career than to increase the number of discoveries, but his cup of joy is full when the result of his observations is put to immediate practical use."
Louis Pasteur.

Director of Scientific Studies.

It was now that Louis came up against that old idea – it had lain in wait for him for a century since Spallanzani's efforts to finish it off – the theory of *spontaneous generation*.

Scientists no longer believed that humans, animals, or insects, were produced *except* by parents of their own kind. But many believed that among microbes – fungi, yeasts, and other micro-organisms – spontaneous generation did happen.

Everything in his fermentation work led Louis to the belief that microbes are already in the air, and that we only notice them, with a microscope, when they land on solid matter or dive into liquids. He was not alone in believing this. Others, like his old teachers Biot and Dumas, rejected spontaneous generation.

But Louis Pasteur was never happy with anything

Fashionable Paris. Louis once wrote to his father, "Here, more than anywhere, we see vice and virtue, honesty and dishonesty, riches and poverty, perpetually colliding and interweaving. But one can remain simple and upright in heart, here as well as anywhere." Louis could have become immensely wealthy from the proceeds of pasteurization and vaccines, for he saved the alcohol brewers and many farmers from disaster. He chose instead to give the income from his work to the State or to spend it on necessary scientific equipment. Throughout his life, his devotion was to science and its benefits for society.

Left: Louis' first "laboratory" at the Ecole Normale was two attic rooms at the top of the building – the only unused space he could find. Later he moved into slightly bigger rooms in this building by the gate. Here he and his assistants did nearly all the work on the microbes of disease.

Professor Jean-Baptiste Biot, Louis' physics professor, and one of his long-standing supporters. Like many others, he agreed with Louis that "spontaneous generation" was nonsense; but he also felt that it would be impossible to prove, and Louis was probably wasting his time. Louis disagreed, and he was not only a skilled scientist but also obstinately single-minded in pursuit of an idea which he felt deserved to be tested. He ignored the advice of the much more experienced Professor Biot, and pressed on.

Biot was delighted to be proved wrong.

less than something he could prove beyond a doubt. As an old man, he was to say, "If I had to live my life over again, I would try always to remember that admirable precept of Bossuet: 'The greatest disorder of the mind is to believe that things are so because we wish them to be so.'"

On the brink of the most decisive conviction of his career, he knew there was only one way to go on: proof and only proof would shift scientists in the direction he believed they must go.

Fermentation and putrefaction – rotting – never took place unless microbes were present. That much he had proved. But it was generally believed that the microbes in, for example, corpses and rotten meat were caused *by the rotting.* No one saw it the other way round, that the microbes themselves *caused* the rotting. Yet everything in Louis' researches pointed to that conclusion. But how to prove it?

The quest for <u>proof</u>

First he must find a way to show that microbes get into things from the outside. He must kill all the microbes in a sealed container, and show that no new ones appeared. Louis set about devising an experiment, very like Spallanzani's all those years ago. He filled glass flasks with sugary yeast soup and boiled each flask to kill any microbes in it; while it boiled he sealed it by melting the glass at the tip of the neck.

Then he divided the sealed flasks into two groups. He snapped off the tip of the necks of one group with pincers, and allowed air in, then he sealed them again by melting the glass. All the flasks in the second group *he kept sealed.* Then he put both groups in his incubating oven to keep warm enough for any microbes to grow.

The results were unmistakable. In the flasks he had opened and then resealed, yeasts and other fungi grew. In the flasks he had left sealed, nothing grew. Then he did it all over again, again and again and again: flasks of milk, urine, blood: heated, sealed, opened, incubated, just to try and prove himself wrong.

He had proved the germs came only from the outside. But the spontaneous generation supporters retaliated. Cutting off the air, they said, stopped spontaneous generation; microbes needed *natural* unheated air to burst into spontaneous life!

Louis shot a restrained return arrow. "In my opinion, the question is wholly undecided. It is virgin territory and awaits the application of decisive proofs. What is there in the air which gives rise to these creatures? Are they germs? Or a solid substance? Or a fluid? Or a gas? All this is unknown, and we have to *experiment* to find the answers."

The final proof

And while his opponents pronounced on the subject, he went on to devise just such an experiment. He was convinced that it was not the air itself, but the *dusts* in the air that carried the microbes. But try as he might, he couldn't find a way to let air into his flasks, without also letting microbes in.

He was rescued by Professor Balard, an elderly chemistry professor who liked to wander round the laboratories having a look at others' work.

One day he strolled into Louis' laboratory and found him wrestling with his predicament. Like Biot, Dumas and others, Professor Balard agreed with Louis about germs and air, and thought it would be a fine thing to prove it. So he put his chemist's brain to the problem of Louis' flasks and his dustless air, and came up with the solution: prepare the flasks, then heat and bend the necks in a long downward S-shape. Air would be able to pass along it, but dust would fall downwards with the force of gravity and would not be able to travel round the bends ...

Excitedly Louis did this. Again he prepared his yeast soup and boiled it. As the liquid boiled, the air was forced out: but this time as the liquid cooled, the air was drawn in, *but the dust and the microbes stuck in the long curving neck.* The flasks remained clear, without contamination by microbes. Yet when he shook some so that the clear yeast soup flooded

The original swan-necked flasks used by Louis in his experiments on germs in the air; today they can be seen in the Pasteur Institute in Paris – still germ-free a hundred-and-thirty years after he first performed the experiment!

into the swan-necks, picking up the dust, then back into the belly of the flask, they became filled with microbes, multiplying gleefully!

Even today, over a century later, the swan-necked flasks are still clear, still proving the simple truth of Louis' experiment and the simple generosity of scientists like Professor Balard, who only wanted the truth to emerge.

The search for pure air again

Louis reasoned that the amount of dust in the air would vary in different places; surely there would be more in a busy street in Paris than at the top of a mountain? His next task must be to show that there were different amounts of *microbes* in the air in these different places.

By now he had assistants helping him: together they prepared their sealed flasks of yeast soup and carried ten to the cellars of the Paris Observatory, ten more to the yard of the Observatory, twenty

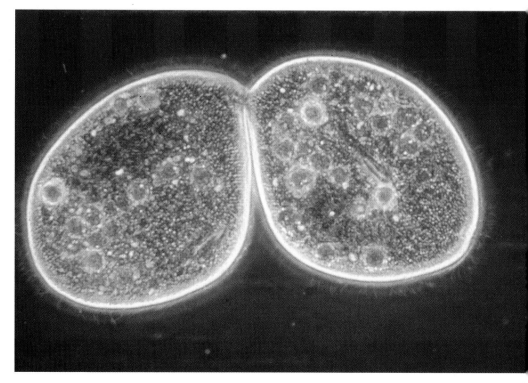

up a hill near Louis' home-town of Arbois, and twenty more up Mont Blanc.

Of the ten flasks opened in the cellars, where the air was still and Louis predicted there would be little dust, only one developed microbes. In the yard ten out of ten went bad. On the hill near Arbois, only eight out of twenty grew microbes, and on another, higher hill, only five out of twenty. And out of the twenty flasks taken up Mont Blanc, only one developed microbes.

In November 1860, Louis told the Academy of Science of his results. "They enable us, in my opinion, to state definitely that the dusts suspended in the atmosphere are the exclusive origin, the initial, indispensable condition for the existence of life in the liquids."

He added, with his unfailing sense of vision, "What would be most desirable of all would be to carry these studies far enough to prepare the way for serious research into the origin of different diseases."

Like other scientists before him, Louis Pasteur observed that many microbes increase simply by dividing. But the depth of his understanding of this process was at the heart of his visionary perception of how to control disease. A single organism could, within seven or eight hours, become millions, and a picture took root in his mind of different types of microbe doing battle with each other for control – the winner overrunning the substance or body it inhabited. In this photograph, one of the micro-organisms known as protozoa is in the final stages of division into two micro-organisms.

Top: Louis and his wife, in 1889.
Bottom: Louis with his granddaughter. Three of his five children died – two from typhoid fever.
We can only guess how this must have fired his fierce determination to unravel the mystery of disease.

Years of dedication

And so Louis Pasteur had launched himself and the scientists of his time on this voyage of discovery. He did his experiments – these, and a thousand others, all with the same clarity and persistence.

Over the next ten years, (the argument went on, often bitterly, for many years) he demolished all the objections of his opponents. There was much opposition to him, some on scientific grounds, some because several firmly established scientists wished to oppose this confident young man who blasted into their midst with the air of being right – from the top of his head to the tip of his toes.

But Louis performed his meticulous experiment in public for the Academy of Science, and was seen to be right.

In 1862, when he was nearly forty, he was elected to the Academy; his life was now filled with lectures which fired the imagination of his fellow scientists. So many of them were ripe for this prophet in their midst, and eager to grasp the weapons of understanding he handed them ...

Exciting years, these years of the 1850s and 1860s, for science, for the world! But quietly, in Louis' private life, they were also years of bitter tragedy. In September of 1859, his eldest daughter Jeanne had died suddenly from typhoid fever. She was only nine years old. We are not told much about the events surrounding this tragedy. But who knows what deep core of determination may not have grown from this loss, and helped to propel this extraordinary man forward in his crusade to find the key to control disease?

Germs, germs, everywhere

He decided that the world at large must learn about germs! April of 1864 found him speaking in the Sorbonne to a large audience of scientists, students, ministers of state, famous authors and a princess. He plunged the hall into darkness. Then he shone a beam of light across the room to show millions of dust particles suspended in the air. He spoke to his spellbound listeners of the drifting multitudes of germs within ...

And he showed his two flasks, one with its yeast soup cloudy with microbes and the other with its yeast soup still clear, four years after he had performed the experiment: the soup was still protected from the germs in the dust by the long curving neck of the flask.

"What is the difference between the two?" he asked his fascinated audience. "They are full of the same liquid, they are full of the same air, they are both open. The only difference is this: in this one, the dust of the air and its germs can fall into the flask and reach the liquid and produce microscopic beings. In this other it is impossible, or very difficult, for the germs of the air to reach the liquid."

Not content with converting the world to the germ theory, Louis turned wine doctor too. The winemakers of his home-town of Arbois were having problems. Some of the wine went sour, like

An engraving from the French science magazine La Nature in 1884, showing Louis Pasteur at work in his bare laboratory at the Ecole Normale. By this time the work of Louis Pasteur and his assistants in these simple rooms was propelling fellow scientists forward in a great leap from which they would never return. For the first time, the microbes of disease could be not only tracked and caught, but also fought.

Louis' development of pasteurization saved the French wine industry from disaster. He experimented with heating wine until he discovered that between 50° and 60°C the harmful microbes were killed, but the wine was not spoiled. Later he applied these principles to vinegar and beer. The same pasteurization principles are still used in the alcohol industries.

Opposite: Operating rooms in the middle of the nineteenth century were little more than places of death. Fifty out of a hundred patients died after operations; ten or twenty women out of every hundred died in childbirth from infections caught in the hospital.

vinegar, and would not keep for any length of time. Louis turned his microscope on the wine, and discovered the culprits – the microbes lurking in the vats which made the wine sour, and others which made it bitter. He experimented until he could tell the winemakers exactly how much to heat the wine, just after it had finished fermenting, to kill these microbes without damaging the wine itself. He had invented *pasteurization*.

The germ theory is applied

In Scotland a far-sighted doctor by the name of Joseph Lister, Professor of Surgery in Edinburgh, read of Pasteur's proof of germs in the air. Here was what he had been searching for, in the struggle to control infection in hospitals. Experimenting swiftly with ways of killing germs, he brought about a transformation that was little short of a miracle.

Hospitals were grim places: stinking with the smell of suppurating wounds, pus and blood. More often than not, people died not from the illnesses they had come in with, but from infections they

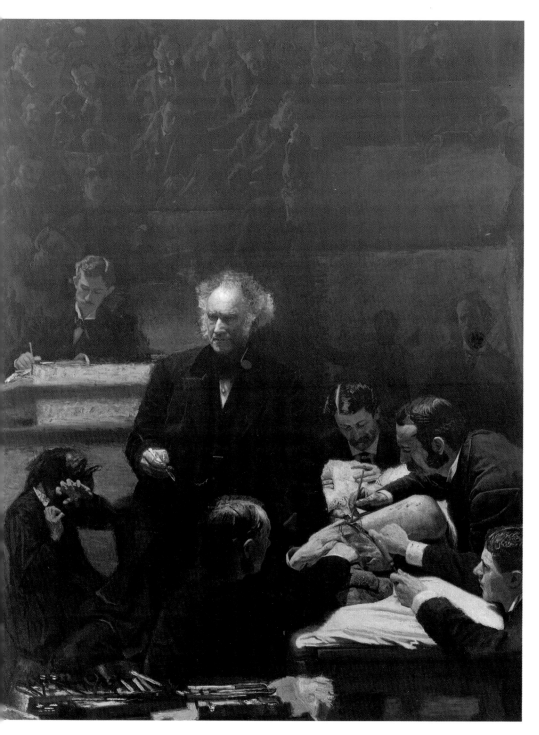

43

Joseph Lister, who first applied Louis Pasteur's proofs of the germ theory of disease. In the years following the introduction of antiseptic surgery, led by Lister, the rate of deaths fell from fifty to five out of one hundred.

"If ever you come to Edinburgh, I think you will find it truly rewarding to walk round our hospital and see how greatly mankind is benefitting from your work. Need I add how great a satisfaction I would derive myself from showing you how much the art of surgery is in your debt."

Joseph Lister, in a letter to Pasteur, 1874.

developed once there. The death rate after operations was very high. Many of Lister's patients seemed to be getting better, but about the fourth day they would develop infection in the wound, and die not long after.

But by 1867, in Lister's wards, all the instruments and equipment used to dress wounds were dipped in a strong solution of carbolic acid to destroy germs, medical workers scrubbed their hands with carbolic acid and a carbolic acid spray played on the wound during the operation. Later the wound was washed with carbolic solution and Lister used antiseptic materials for dressings.

At least fifty out of every hundred once died after operations. Even in the early trials of his new methods, he reduced the death rate to fifteen out of every hundred, and then to three out of every hundred.

Years later, in 1874, he wrote a letter to Louis Pasteur. "Allow me," Lister said, "to take this opportunity to tender you my most cordial thanks for having, by your brilliant researches, demonstrated to me the truth of the germ theory of putrefaction, ... furnishing me with the principles upon which alone the antiseptic system can be carried out."

The change began later in France, when a surgeon after the Franco-Prussian war of 1871 absorbed Pasteur's ideas and wondered if germs were causing the decay that settled into the soldiers' wounds. He began disinfecting instruments and filtering the air around wounds.

The germ theory of disease, again

But the question of what caused disease in the body as a whole, was still open. Doctors mainly believed that disease was "in us and of us and brought into being by us". But the idea that disease and rotting were connected was also an old one. Two hundred years before Pasteur, the English scientist Robert Boyle said, "He that thoroughly understands the nature of ferments and fermentations, shall probably be much better able than he that ignores them, to give a fair account of diverse phenomena of several diseases."

Now Louis, this man who understood ferments, was pushed by an unexpected combination of circumstances to take his first steps along the path which opened those floodgates of knowledge.

The silkworm doctor

It began in 1865. His old friend, Professor Dumas, asked him to go to the south of France, to Dumas' own village of Alais, and investigate the epidemic that was killing the silkworms. It was devastating the famous silk industry, bringing ruin to the people there.

Louis was reluctant to go. But Dumas was an old friend, and so Louis set off with one of his best pupils, Duclaux, three other students from the Ecole Normale, and Madame Pasteur, ever-prepared to turn her hand to whatever this extraordinary husband might do. And of course the family went too. In a cottage in Alais they settled down to solve the tragic mystery caused by the unknown silkworm disease.

Weaving silk in a London cottage. Louis' researches into silkworm disease were of major importance to the silk industries of many countries. He saved many working families, who depended for their living on healthy silkworms spinning their silken cocoons, from destitution. But his silkworm work also had great significance scientifically. It showed what Louis had long predicted – that some kinds of disease are caused by microbes entering a body, and that these microbes can be passed from one generation to the next.

Reeling Cocoons.

Weaving.

Clothing.

The silkworm disease had already devastated the silk industries of Italy, Spain, Austria and even China, where the silk industry was two thousand years old. In southern France, the silkworms' miserable plight was bringing ruin to the region.

The disease seemed to start on the surface of the silkworms, like a dusting of pepper-grains. Here in the south of France it was called *pébrine*, from *pébré*, the local name for pepper.

Hundreds of silk chrysalises and moths went under Louis' microscope. Within a few days he decided that a little globule seen in diseased worms, moths and chrysalises was a *sure sign* of the disease. He decided that it started with mature moths producing diseased eggs which developed into diseased worms, chrysalises and moths.

Conclusion for the silkworm breeders? Check the moth, after she had laid eggs, for any globules in her body. If there are, then the eggs would be diseased and must be destroyed. If the moth's body is clear of globules, the eggs would be sound, and healthy worms would emerge.

Disaster!

He had to wait till the eggs hatched in the spring to find out if his predictions were right. And now Louis learned a bitter lesson. Spring came; the eggs he thought came from healthy moths produced diseased worms; hundreds of silkworm breeders, relying on his method of sorting eggs, faced disaster.

He had made a dreadful mistake; back he went to his microscope to find where the mistake was. He struggled; he tried experiments that didn't work, and he couldn't understand why: there were dying worms which didn't have globules, and live worms that did. He felt terribly responsible, and suffered bitter attacks from the breeders and his enemies.

But his pupils were not discouraged. They went on with the experiments he asked them to do, and the work continued, month after month.

It was an epic of scientific investigation and struggle. In the end they found where the mistake had been: there were two diseases, not one, one with globules, and one with another microscopic creature, quite different. They had learned a vital fact about the *pébrine* globule: it was alive. It was a microbe. It multiplied, spreading throughout the moth, egg or worm.

Louis was totally ignorant of silkworms. He was amazed, when given his first cocoon, to find that something rattled inside when he shook it. With some fascination he learned that this was the chrysalis, the creature that the silkworm becomes before turning into a moth; the silkworm spins the silken cocoon to protect this chrysalis, and it is from this cocoon that the chrysalis-turned moth climbs to lay eggs which hatch out into new silkworms.

Above: A silk moth on silk cocoons.
Left: Silkworms feeding on mulberry leaves.
Below left: A silk moth emerging from the chrysalis.

Opposite: At the height of cholera epidemics, hundreds of people died each day in Paris alone. In 1865, Pasteur and others tried to find out if the outbreak was caused by a microbe. They sampled the air of the cholera wards and took blood from patients ... but got nowhere. They tried again in an epidemic in Egypt in 1883, but failed. It was Robert Koch who finally showed that cholera is caused by a microbe spread through infected drinking water. The most essential method of control is good sanitation.

So Louis saved the people of the silkworm lands who depended on these little creatures spinning their silken cocoons. He learned how vital it was to be unfailingly methodical and complete in his work. He had found out also that healthy worms became sick when the droppings from sick worms soiled the mulberry leaves they ate: the second disease that had confused him, *flacherie*, was passed on through the worms' intestines. In effect he showed the importance of the environment in spreading disease.

Vital new ideas! Disease must have been very much on people's minds in those years. Cholera had broken out in Paris and Marseilles: people were dying at the rate of two hundred a day.

Sorrow takes a crippling toll

Disease must have been on Louis' mind in a very personal way too. He had already lost his eldest daughter Jeanne, dead from typhoid fever. In September of 1865 the baby of the family, his two-year-old daughter, Camille, became ill and died.

Only a few months later Cécile, twelve years old, also fell victim to typhoid fever. By May of 1866, she too was dead.

It took an appalling toll on Louis: the terrible frustration of seeing that the doctors could not save his children, the problems of his own work on the silkworms, the sense of responsibility to people who depended for their survival on him getting his conclusions right. In October of 1868, he was back in Paris. On the nineteenth he woke up feeling rather strange: all down his left side there was a tingling sensation.

By afternoon he was convulsed with shivering, but he had promised to read a note to the Academy of Science that evening on behalf of an Italian scientist. When he came home, he went to bed, still feeling ill. During the night, his condition worsened. He could no longer speak or move. The whole of his left side was paralyzed.

He was nearly forty-six, and he had had a stroke. They thought he was going to die.

Le Petit Journal

ADMINISTRATION
61, RUE LAFAYETTE, 61

Les manuscrits ne sont pas rendus

On s'abonne sans frais
dans tous les bureaux de poste

5 CENT.

SUPPLÉMENT ILLUSTRÉ

23me Année

DIMANCHE 1er DÉCEMBRE 1912

5 CENT.

Numéro 1.150

ABONNEMENTS

	SIX MOIS	UN AN
SEINE et SEINE-ET-OISE.	2 fr.	3 fr. 50
DÉPARTEMENTS.	2 fr.	4 fr. »
ÉTRANGER	2 50	5 fr. »

LE CHOLÉRA

Louis Pasteur, with members of his team. After Louis' stroke in 1868, which paralyzed half his body, he became dependent on others to perform the detailed experiments he planned. Many other great scientists emerged from these close partnerships with Louis.

He had to fight ignorance, prejudice, the innate conservatism of his eminent colleagues and of the medical establishment. He fought this fight, with kindness, good humour, and a basic equanimity, which yet allowed the passion of his 'exalted mind' to drive him on and to inspire other ... men with some of his own enthusiasm."

H.I. Winner, from "Louis Pasteur and Microbiology".

Recovery

But Louis Pasteur would defy predictions. He managed to speak again, at first only single words, and then fully. A week later he was dictating notes to his assistants. But he was paralyzed in the left arm and leg. He refused to let it stop him working. Within three months he was off to Alais to see how the silkworm work was progressing.

From this time on he couldn't handle the scientific apparatus himself so he became dependent on his assistants to perform the careful manipulations in the experiments he devised. Many great scientists were born out of these close partnerships with Louis Pasteur, infected by his style, filled with his enthusiasm and his unfailing strength of spirit.

The more he studied silkworms the more certain Pasteur became of a link between the fermentations of yeasts, disease in animals and humans. Again he sounded his clarion call to his fellows: "It is in the power of man to make parasitic illnesses disappear from the face of the globe, if the doctrine of spontaneous generation is wrong, as I am sure it is."

Yet doctors as a body dismissed these predictions: epidemic diseases, due just to a microbe! Nonsense! It was a country doctor in Germany who turned these predictions into fact, and stopped for all time the doubts about the significance of what Louis Pasteur had shown.

One microbe, one disease

In East Prussia, in the heart of farm country, there was a man named Robert Koch who wanted to be an explorer but had become a doctor, and was frustrated by his inability to do anything to cure disease.

But he was given a microscope for his birthday by his wife, who hoped it would help to quieten his restlessness. One day Koch turned his microscope on the gluey black blood from animals that had died of anthrax, a disease that was wiping out whole herds of sheep and cattle throughout Europe. At once Koch saw the rod-like microbes swarming in the sick blood ...

Following his curious nose, and his restless

explorer's instinct, with a thousand tests and experiments and then a thousand more, Koch proved that the rod-like things were alive. Then he proved they multiplied, they were never found in healthy animals, they could survive shrivelled into spores, lurking until they could burst into activity again, that the anthrax microbe *(bacillus anthracis)*, and this alone, caused the disease of anthrax.

In April of 1876, three years after he had started work on the problem, he went to see his old professors and told them about it. There it was: *one microbe caused one disease.* Pasteur had said it repeatedly, and suggested it in the silkworm disease. Koch had proved it.

Now the hunt was on for the microbes that had been slaughtering people year after year and still were: cholera, typhoid, tuberculosis, pneumonia, syphilis, diphtheria, the Russian plague ... in the decades that followed all were the focus of scientists' prying lenses, trying to track down the microbes, grow them, and learn how they lived and died ...

Koch had proved the cause and Pasteur now set his heart to search for the cure.

The dawn of immunology

With increasing clarity during these years, Louis saw disease as a form of struggle for existence, a contest between the microbe and the tissues they try to invade.

During his travels around France he had seen a cow that had anthrax but had recovered naturally from it; he had seen that the cow did not then die when injected with powerful anthrax bacilli. The idea took root in his mind that having the disease somehow caused the body to develop a resistance against it. There the idea lurked, waiting for the moment to blossom forth ...

Louis was not a doctor, and there were many doctors who thought that laboratory scientists like him should not be meddling in medicine. But there were enough who recognised the impact that Pasteur's researches were having, and in 1873 he was elected to the Academy of Medicine.

He took on some young doctors as his assistants,

Robert Koch first proved what Louis Pasteur had been predicting for years – that a specific microbe causes a specific disease. He developed four essential steps for proving this: first find the same microbe in every case of the disease. Second, isolate the microbe and grow it outside the body. Third, inject the newly-grown microbes into an animal and create the disease again. Fourth, remove the microbe from the infected animal and repeat the process until there is no doubt that only this is the cause.

Dr. Joubert, Dr. Roux and Dr. Chamberland. They brought that extra knowledge of the human and animal body and the techniques of medical practice; more and more Pasteur's work turned to the search for control of disease-causing microbes.

Chance – and the greatest breakthrough

In 1878 he began studying the microbe which caused a poultry disease called chicken cholera. It had recently killed a tenth of the chickens in France. Pasteur was growing the microbes in chicken broth, and had seen that when injected into chickens, it killed them within days.

It was summertime: Louis and his assistants went on holiday, and a culture of chicken cholera microbes was put to one side and forgotten. On returning, Louis was about to throw it away when he changed his mind and decided to inject it into a hen.

In went a syringeful. The hen became mildly sick, but recovered quickly. By the time hens usually showed signs of the disease she was still well! And in the days that followed she stayed well, happily strutting around her cage.

Opposite, top: bacillus anthracis – the microbe which causes anthrax in animals and can kill them within hours. People can also die from it. They can catch it from animal hair and hides: shepherds, butchers, farmers, even meat porters or women wearing furs from diseased animals were at great risk. The bacilli grow in long chains, as shown in this picture.

Opposite, bottom: bacillus anthracis shown in animal tissue. In humans it attacks the lungs or causes skin ulcers. Developing the vaccine was dangerous work for Louis and his assistants, a scratch might be enough to kill.

Excited, (for he remembered the cow that had not died of anthrax), Louis injected more hens with the old culture. They joined the first in strutting smugly around the cages. His brain aflame with what he dared to hope was happening, he injected them with a fresh culture, strong enough to kill. Each hen got the killer dose.

They were unaffected. He injected the fresh culture into another batch of hens, that had *not* been inoculated with the old culture. They all died.

"In the field of experimentation chance favours the prepared mind", Louis once said. He understood immediately what this all meant: an English doctor named Edward Jenner had used the microbes of the mild disease of cowpox to vaccinate against smallpox, and this was now widely used in Europe.

But Jenner's methods were based on using a disease known *not to be harmful to people,* to produce protection against a disease which *was* dangerous.

What was happening with chicken cholera was

different. *Weakened* microbes of the disease itself had raised the hen's own defences so she could fight off the disease.

Could it be done again? His mind buzzed with the problems. And one by one, by experimenting, he answered all the questions. He decided to call the treatment *vaccination* after Jenner's methods: and we still use the term now for this technique of preventing a disease by inoculating in advance against it, by *immunisation.*

How many other microbes could be grown in the laboratory, weakened, and used as vaccines? What excitement he must have felt!

For so long he had called for this and worked for it. And the rest of his life would be devoted to long and laborious searches for ways of weakening the ability of microbes to multiply, weakening them enough not to cause the disease, but enough to force the body's natural defences to arm themselves.

The anthrax vaccine

For some time Louis had also been studying the disease of anthrax, on which Koch had already done such magnificent work. Scientists knew what caused it, but still the cattle-rearing provinces of France were losing thousands of cattle each year, sheep flocks were devastated, sometimes as many as half dying. People also died from it – a scratch was enough to kill.

The search for an anthrax vaccine took many years. Pasteur and his team started work on anthrax in 1877: in 1879 they made the chicken cholera discovery. Not until February of 1881 did Louis believe they had succeeded with anthrax vaccine.

The great challenge

He accepted a challenge from the farmers in Melun, near Paris, to test it in public. It is famous, that day in May of 1881, at the farm of Pouilly-le-Fort. Ministers of state, animal doctors and farmers, scientists, reporters, even from England, gathered to see Louis and his assistants, Roux, Chamberland and Thuillier – and the sheep.

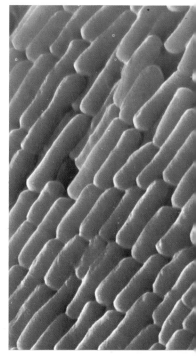

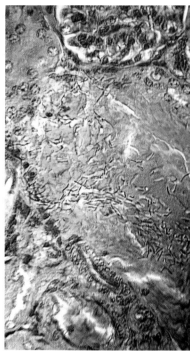

A drawing from a French magazine of 1882 showing a doctor vaccinating sheep according to Louis Pasteur's method. In Pasteur's own words, "The general principles have been found and one cannot refuse to believe that the future is rich with the greatest hopes."

"Your father is as preoccupied as ever; he hardly speaks to me, sleeps little, and rises at dawn; in short, he is leading the same life as I began sharing with him, thirty-five years ago today."

Madame Pasteur, in a letter to her children on her wedding anniversary, 1884.

Twenty-five sheep received two vaccinations with weakened microbes – first with very old, weak ones, then twelve days later with fresher, stronger ones, to build up their resistance. Another twenty-five received no vaccinations at all. The two groups were kept in separate fields. Then all fifty were given fatal doses of powerful anthrax microbes.

Publicly confident, Louis was privately consumed with nerves, unable to sleep, unable to open the telegram from Pouilly-le-Fort, telling the results. Madame Pasteur had to open it for him, her own hands trembling. Government officials, scientists, farmers, gathered, buzzing, while the numbers were counted and counted again ... All the vaccinated were healthy. All the unvaccinated were dead or dying. What a roar of welcome greeted Pasteur and his fellow workers as they arrived at Melun!

Within no time Pasteur's laboratories were turned over to making the vaccine, and the tireless Roux, Chamberland and Thuillier rushed across France injecting animals, till they saw injection syringes in their sleep. In under a year hundreds of thousands of animals were vaccinated: in the following year in France alone half a million sheep and eighty thousand oxen.

There were problems with the vaccine. They had difficulty making it pure enough; sometimes it caused anthrax; sometimes it just didn't work. But the giant leap in medical knowledge was undeniable: a vaccine had been prepared which could prevent, *in advance*, a disease which devastated farming areas throughout Europe.

His final crusade

Many people remember Pasteur more for his cure for rabies. It was a terrible disease: a bite from a rabid dog or wolf and the victim would begin to shake, feel they were being strangled, and either die from suffocation or be paralyzed.

The victims of rabies always went mad: Louis and his team reasoned that the microbe was probably in the central nervous system.

They took nerve tissue – fragments from the spinal cord of a mad dog which had died from rabies – and injected it into a rabbit. A fortnight later the rabbit had rabies. They took some of its spinal cord, when it died, and injected it into another rabbit; and so on, until it had been transferred twenty-five times, and the time for the disease to develop had become shorter, until it was only a week. Then they took a fragment of infected spinal marrow and looked for ways of weakening it.

By March of 1885 Louis wrote to a friend, "I have demonstrated this year that one can vaccinate dogs or render them immune to rabies. I have not dared to treat humans bitten by rabid dogs."

The boy with rabies

One Monday morning – July 6, 1885 – nine-year-old Joseph Meister arrived at Pasteur's laboratory with his mother. He had been savaged in his village in Alsace two days before by a mad dog – bitten on face, hands and body.

What was Pasteur to do? The vaccine wasn't ready for human tests. He asked colleagues from

Pasteur's search for a rabies cure took over three years. He could not find the microbe: we now know it is a virus and a more powerful microscope is needed to detect things as small. First Louis and his assistants took spinal cord from a dog which had died from rabies and injected it from rabbit to rabbit to shorten the time for rabies to develop. Then they looked for ways of weakening the microbes.

"If the animal screamed at all, Pasteur was immediately filled with compassion, and tried to comfort and encourage the victim, in a way that would have seemed ludicrous if it had not been touching."
Dr. Emile Roux

The shepherd-boy Jupille, being inoculated against rabies. After much trial and error, their method of injecting the weakened anthrax microbes was: first day, inject fourteen-day-old dried tissue, next day inject thirteen-day-old tissue, injecting fresher microbes each day, until on the fourteenth day, fresh living microbes were used.

"Even granted that the antirabies treatment had saved the lives of a few human beings, this would have been only meagre return for so much effort, and for so many animals sacrificed on the altar of man's welfare. ... It is on much broader issues that Pasteur's achievements must be judged. ... Thanks to the rabies epic, men were to be immunized against yellow fever and several other widespread virus diseases; even more important, immunisation had become recognized as a general law of nature. Its importance for the welfare of man and animals is today commonplace, but only the future will reveal its full significance in the realm of human economy."
Professor René J. Dubos, from "Free Lance of Science".

the Academy of Medicine: would the boy develop rabies? They counted his fourteen deep wounds, and said he would. Yet Pasteur's vaccine might kill him. If Pasteur did not inoculate him there was a good chance Joseph would die anyway, or be completely paralyzed.

Louis decided to take the plunge. On the evening of July 6 he supervised a doctor injecting the extract from the weakened spinal cord of a rabbit which had died of rabies fifteen days before. Over the next ten days, more injections were given, each day with a stronger extract. Joseph's bites healed and he never contracted rabies.

The news of his cure flashed round the world. From all over Europe, farmers and peasants who had been bitten by rabid dogs and wolves flooded into Paris for Pasteur's treatment.

We will never know how many survived because of Pasteur's vaccine, for rabies doesn't always kill its victims. But many of them would have died. That crucial jump had been made: *from animals to humans.* The Academy of Science decided to

Above: Louis' rooms at the Pasteur Institute in Paris, where he spent most of his last years. Left: This statue of Joseph Meister wrestling with the dog which savaged him stands in the grounds of the Pasteur Institute in Paris. It commemorates the leap in medical knowledge: from vaccines for animals, to vaccines for humans. Louis had seen the suffering from rabies – when he was a boy a rabid wolf had terrorized Arbois. He had watched the victims being seared by red hot irons, and he never forgot the smell of scorching flesh, or the look of madness.

Dr. Emile Roux, one of Pasteur's assistants, injecting a horse during his investigations on the toxins, or poisons, of diphtheria.

Elie Metchnikov, one of Pasteur's most brilliant pupils, began to unravel the ways in which the body fights back against microbes, and develops immunity against them.

found an institute to be called the Pasteur Institute, to organize the treatment of rabies.

The world responded: money poured in.

Pasteur's final years

Louis continued working until he was nearly seventy. In 1887, when he was sixty-four, another paralytic stroke prevented him from personally doing experimental work, but his dialogue with his pupils and his collaborators, never ceased. In November 1888, the Pasteur Institute was officially opened, and he was able to see them continue in the spirit of enthusiasm and determination which had been the guiding impetus of his own life.

He died on September 28, 1895, when he was seventy-two, surrounded by family, colleagues and students. For nearly half a century he had dominated the scientific world; for a quarter of a century he had surged onward despite a half-paralysis of his body. Now the body was dead. But the spirit was not; it lived on in the scientists and doctors who inherited the knowledge he bequeathed.

Pasteur's legacy

The young men he had trained went on to new glories. Dr. Roux and Dr. Yersin developed the treatment for diphtheria which once killed thousands of children every year. Metchnikov, one of Pasteur's most brilliant assistants, would begin to lay bare the ways in which the body develops a resistance to microbes and develops immunity.

Dr. Yersin discovered the microbe that causes the plague. But when Pasteur, old and retired, had looked through the microscope at it, his only comment had been, "Ah, what a lot there is still to do!"

It is too easy to talk of Pasteur the genius who did it all, and too easy to say that if he hadn't someone else would have. Nothing is achieved by single effort: all is a part of the times in which people live and the accumulation of knowledge brought about by many, so that it is possible to draw together the strands and push forward the frontiers, as did Pasteur.

Joseph Lister greeting Louis Pasteur at the celebrations for his seventieth birthday at the Sorbonne. Pasteur is leaning on the arm of the President of the French Republic.

But there is also the man, and who knows what might have been if Pasteur had not been the fighter he was, with that fierce determination to bring about the changes he believed in. And what if other visionary men, like Joseph Lister, had not recognized the truth when they saw it and produced the revolution around Pasteur's work?

Pasteur had once said to his students, "You bring me the deepest joy that can be felt by a man whose invincible belief it is that science and peace will triumph over ignorance and war ... that the future will belong to those who will have done most for suffering humanity."

One wonders, thinking of the enormous life of Louis Pasteur, if his last words to Madame Pasteur as she offered him a drink, "I can't", were perhaps the first time he had ever truly entertained the notion of failure.

"You have raised the veil that for all the centuries made infectious illness a dark mystery."
Joseph Lister, to Louis Pasteur, at his Jubilee.

59

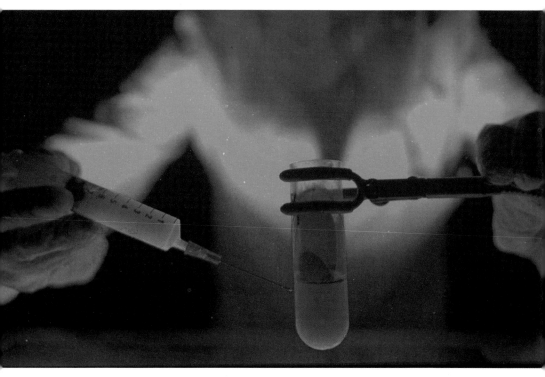

A recent experiment at the Pasteur Institute. The Institute has become the most famous centre for the study of microbes and microbial diseases. It has prompted the foundation of such institutes all over the world, and it trains its microbiologists to continue in the forefront of research to conquer disease. It is one of the great foundations of the scientific and medical revolution which in this century has led to routine vaccines for children for polio, diphtheria, tetanus, measles, as well as vaccines against the great epidemic diseases of typhoid, tuberculosis and cholera. The Pasteur Institute continues to break new ground in microbial research and the AIDS virus was discovered there.

Glossary

Anthrax: A highly infectious disease of cattle and sheep which can be transmitted to humans. Symptoms include fever and a swollen throat. It is almost always fatal, unless vaccine is immediately available.

Antiseptic: A substance that kills or inhibits the growth of disease-causing *micro-organisms*, but essentially is not poisonous to the body.

Asepsis: The absence of germs and the way of achieving a *germ*-free condition in surgery.

Bacillus: [Plural: bacilli] Any rod-shaped *bacterium*.

Bacterium: [Plural: bacteria] Any one of a large group of single-celled *micro-organisms*. Some cause disease. They are mostly responsible for the decay of dead plants and animals.

Carbolic acid: A poisonous white acid, made from petroleum, which is used as an *antiseptic*.

Cholera: A serious intestine illness caused by drinking water containing the cholera *microbe* transmitted by human or animal faeces. Its symptoms include severe diarrhoea and stomach cramps. In the 1832 French *epidemic*, the death rate was twenty-three in every thousand people.

Chrysalis: The third stage in the life of a butterfly or moth. During it, the insect changes into the adult form.

Cocoon: A silky protective

covering spun by a silkworm to protect its *chrysalis*.

Crystal: A structure with a regular shape, in which the sides intersect at regular angles.

Culture: The growing of *micro-organisms* in a suitable medium under controlled conditions. Can also mean the resulting colony of micro-organisms.

Diphtheria: A very infectious disease caused by a *bacillus*. Diphtheria often used to be fatal in small children.

Dissymmetry: The relationship between two objects when one is the mirror image of the other.

Epidemic: The widespread occurrence of a disease.

Electron microscope: It can magnify images of structures up to a million times so that the human eye can see them. This is a vastly greater magnification than the light microscopes of Pasteur's day, and because of this they were unable to detect viruses, which we now know cause many diseases.

Fermentation: A process of decomposition (rotting) brought about by *micro-organisms*, especially *bacteria* and *yeasts*.

Pasteur's work caused scientists to divide fermentation into three main areas: **alcoholic** in which alcohol is produced during wine or beer making; **acetic** in which wine and other alcohols are turned into vinegar; and **lactic** in which the sugars in milk are turned into acids – for example when milk goes sour.

Germ: A *micro-organism*; in popular terminology, a *microbe*.

Immunization: To protect against a specific disease usually by *inoculation*.

Incubator: A box or oven which keeps its contents at a constant temperature.

Inoculation: To place a measured dose of a modified *bacillus* or other disease-causing *microbe* into a human or animal in order to cause the body to produce its own defence against the disease. Also called vaccination.

Lactic acid: A syrupy acid found in sour milk and also in some types of fruit.

Latin Quarter: An area of Paris, on the south bank of the River Seine, where the Sorbonne University and other educational establishments are situated.

Maggot: The second (or larval) stage of flies; usually found in rotting substances like meat, after the adult fly has laid its eggs.

Micro-organism: Any creature which is too small to be seen with the naked eye.

Microbe: A *micro-organism*.

Microbiology: The study of *micro-organisms*.

Pasteurization: A process, pioneered by Pasteur, of heating wine, beer, etc to prevent harmful *bacteria* from ruining the *fermentation*. Also used on milk and other foods to destroy harmful bacteria.

Plague: Diseases which cause *epidemics* by being very infectious and causing many deaths.

Pneumonia: An infection of the lungs. The lungs partly fill with liquid, so that the flooded areas cannot be used for breathing. Usually caused by a *virus*.

Prussia: A kingdom lying in modern north-eastern Germany and Poland.

Pus: A greeny-yellow fluid which appears in wounds infected by certain *bacteria;* a clear sign that the wound is not healing properly.

Rabies: A very infectious disease of the nervous system of warm-blooded animals, caused by a *virus*. It is passed on to humans by the bite of an infected animal. Symptoms include convulsions, excessive *saliva* production, and (in humans) an aversion to water.

Before Pasteur developed his vaccine, death or paralysis were the inevitable result of being bitten.

Saliva: The liquid produced by glands in the mouth. Its purpose is to make it easier to swallow food.

Smallpox: A very infectious disease caused by a *virus*. Although not always fatal, this disease was a major killer until well into the twentieth century. It is now eradicated from the world.

Solution: A liquid mixture of two atoms or molecules, where they blend completely.

Spontaneous generation: A discredited scientific theory which held that, given the right conditions, life would appear without any cause.

Stroke: The breaking of a blood vessel in the brain which makes the victim lose consciousness. The result may be paralysis, loss of speech and brain damage.

Sugar-beet: A vegetable from whose large white roots sugar can be extracted.

Tuberculosis: An infectious disease caused by a *bacillus* which mainly attacks the lungs.

Typhoid fever: A very infectious disease, caught by eating or drinking something contaminated by the faeces of someone infected with the *bacillus*.

Vaccination: *see* Inoculation.

Virus: A type of *micro-organism* which can only reproduce within the body of another animal or human. It very often causes a disease.

Yeast: A type of fungus used in the *fermentation* industries and in baking.

Important Dates

1822   Dec 27: Louis Pasteur is born in Dôle, France.

1843   Louis enters the Ecole Normale in fourth place.

1848   Louis reads his paper on crystals to the Academy of Science.

1849   Louis is appointed Lecturer of Chemistry at Strasbourg University.
May 29: Louis marries Marie Laurent, daughter of the university principal.

1853   Louis Pasteur is awarded the Legion d'Honneur. His daughter, Cécile, is born.

1854   Louis, aged only thirty-one, is made Professor of Chemistry and Dean of the new Faculty of Science at Lille.

1856   Louis begins studies on fermentation.

1857   Louis becomes Director of Scientific Studies at the Ecole Normale in Paris.

1859   Their oldest daughter, Jeanne, dies from typhoid fever aged nine. Louis begins studies into spontaneous generation.

1862   Louis is elected to the Academy of Science.

1864   Apr: Louis demonstrates his germ theory at the Sorbonne in Paris.
July: Louis goes to Arbois to test the wine fermentation; he discovers that heating the wine to 50-60°C will prevent it going acid – he invents pasteurization.

1865   June: Louis goes to Alais in southern France to investigate a disease that is killing the silkworms. His father dies suddenly.
Sept: His two-year-old daughter, Camille, dies after a long illness.

1866   May: Twelve-year-old Cécile dies from typhoid fever.

1867   May: Louis is awarded a Grand Prize medal at the Exposition Universelle for his work on pasteurization. He is appointed Professor of Chemistry at the Sorbonne in Paris.

1868   Oct 19: Louis has a stroke. He is forty-five.

1870   The Franco-Prussian war starts.

1871   Louis starts studying beer fermentation.

1873   Louis is elected to the Academy of Medicine.

1876   Louis publishes his "Studies on Beer".

1877   Louis starts studying anthrax after an outbreak in eastern France.

1879   During work on chicken cholera, Louis discovers how to immunize against disease using weakened microbes.

1880   Louis starts studying the disease of rabies.

1881   June 5: Louis' bold experiment vaccinating sheep against anthrax is a complete success. He is awarded the Grand Cross of the Legion d'Honneur.

1885   July 6: Joseph Meister is brought to Louis Pasteur, having been bitten by a rabid dog. Louis decides to vaccinate him – the first person ever to be vaccinated against rabies. He survives and patients come from all over France for treatment.

1888	Nov 14: The Pasteur Institute is officially opened.
1892	Dec 27: A great ceremony is held at the Sorbonne to recognize Louis' achievements.
1894	The Pasteur Institute achieves a vaccination for diphtheria.
1895	Sept 28: Louis dies at Villeneuve L'Etang, aged seventy-two.

Pasteur's legacy

Compared with the centuries of inexplicable disease which had gone before, events moved very swiftly following Pasteur's pioneering work against microbial disease in the 1870s and 1880s. By the end of the century most of the bacteria that caused common diseases had been identified, many of them in Pasteur's laboratory in France and in the laboratories of Robert Koch in Germany.

Even before Pasteur's death in 1895, the first evidence of a disease caused by a virus had been accumulated, although the actual virus had to be guessed at. Not until 1938 was it first seen with the power of an electron microscope.

By the turn of the century, people could be protected against several epidemic diseases, and there were antidotes to the bacterial poisons or toxins of diphtheria and tetanus. (The diphtheria toxin had been isolated by Roux and Yiersin in 1888 at the Pasteur Institute, the tetanus toxin by scientists in Robert Koch's laboratory in 1890.)

In the twentieth century, effective vaccines have been developed against smallpox, tuberculosis, yellow fever, rabies, poliomyelitis, cholera, measles, typhoid, whooping cough, rubella and influenza. There is also a vaccine against the plague.

The major leap of the twentieth century has been the development of the drugs called antibiotics which can destroy infection in the body without harming the person.

After the first use of penicillin in 1941 other antibiotics were swiftly developed, a fitting culmination to the hundred years since Louis Pasteur's first work on fermentation set scientists' feet on that march against disease.

"That enthusiasm which has possessed you from the outset, my dear collaborators – keep it, but let strict verification be its travelling companion. Never put forward an opinion which cannot be simply and decisively proved. Make a cult of the critical spirit. By itself it can neither awaken ideas nor spur the mind to great things. Without it, everything is frail and precarious. Invariably, it has the last word."
Pasteur, to the young scientists of the Institute.

"Young people, trust scientific method, whose first secrets we yet scarcely know. Don't be discouraged. Live in the serene peace of laboratories and libraries. At the end of your life be able to say: I have done what I could."
Louis Pasteur, in his Jubilee speech.

Index

Further Reading

Cuny, Hilaire: *Louis Pasteur: the man and his theories*, Souvenir Press, 1965
Scribener & Co: *Dictionary of Scientific Biography:* article on Louis Pasteur, New York, 1985
Vallery-Radot, Rene: *The Life of Pasteur*, Constable, 1906 (frequently reprinted, an adult biography written by his son-in-law)

JB
Pasteur
Birch
Louis Pasteur

GAYLORD S